The Wiersbe

BIBLE STUDY SERIES

The Wiersbe
BIBLE STUDY SERIES

GALATIANS

Exchange

Legalism

for True

Spirituality

DAVID C COOK

transforming lives together

THE WIERSBE BIBLE STUDY SERIES: GALATIANS
Published by David C Cook
4050 Lee Vance Drive
Colorado Springs, CO 80918 U.S.A.

Integrity Music Limited, a Division of David C Cook
Brighton, East Sussex BN1 2RE, England

The graphic circle C logo is a registered trademark of David C Cook.

ISBN 978-1-4347-6509-3
eISBN 978-0-7814-0377-1

© 2010 Warren W. Wiersbe

The Team: Steve Parolini, Karen Lee-Thorp, Amy Kiechlin,
Sarah Schultz, Jack Campbell, and Karen Athen
Series Cover Design: John Hamilton Design
Cover Photo: Veer Inc.

Printed in the United States of America
First Edition 2010

10 11 12 13 14 15 16 17 18 19

032620

Contents

Introduction to Galatians

Reader Beware

Galatians is a dangerous book.

It exposes the most popular substitute for spiritual living that we have in our churches today—legalism. I didn't say "among false cults." I said "in our churches" because that is where much legalism is today.

Millions of believers think they are "spiritual" because of what they don't do—or because of the leader they follow—or because of the group they belong to. The Lord shows us in Galatians how wrong we are—and how right we can be if only we would let the Holy Spirit take over.

A Battle for Truth

As you begin to read Paul's letter to the Galatian Christians, you can tell immediately that something is radically wrong, because he does not open his letter with his usual elaborate praise to God and prayer for the saints. He has no time! Paul is about to engage in a battle for the truth of the gospel and the liberty of the Christian life. False teachers are spreading a false "gospel," which is a mixture of law and grace, and Paul is not going to stand by and do nothing.

Risk and Reward

So, I say Galatians is a dangerous book. It was dangerous for Paul to write it. It was dangerous for the Galatians to read it. Perhaps my writing this will prove to have been a dangerous thing. (I might lose some friends and some invitations to preach!)

So be it. All I pray is that you and I will appreciate and experience the liberty we have in Christ, lest He have died in vain.

My friend—*Be Free!*

—*Warren W. Wiersbe*

How to Use This Study

This study is designed for both individual and small-group use. We've divided it into eight lessons—each references one or more chapters in Warren W. Wiersbe's commentary *Be Free* (second edition, David C. Cook, 2009). While reading *Be Free* is not a prerequisite for going through this study, the additional insights and background Wiersbe offers can greatly enhance your study experience.

The **Getting Started** questions at the beginning of each lesson offer you an opportunity to record your first thoughts and reactions to the study text. This is an important step in the study process as those "first impressions" often include clues about what it is your heart is longing to discover.

The bulk of the study is found in the **Going Deeper** questions. These dive into the Bible text and, along with helpful excerpts from Wiersbe's commentary, help you examine not only the original context and meaning of the verses but also modern application.

Looking Inward narrows the focus down to your personal story. These intimate questions can be a bit uncomfortable at times, but don't shy away from honesty here. This is where you are asked to stand before the mirror of God's Word and look closely at what you see. It's the place to take a good look at yourself in light of the lesson and search for ways in which you can grow in faith.

Going Forward is the place where you can commit to paper those things you want or need to do in order to better live out the discoveries you made in the Looking Inward section. Don't skip or skim through this. Take the time to really consider what practical steps you might take to move closer to Christ. Then share your thoughts with a trusted friend who can act as an encourager and accountability partner.

Finally, there is a brief **Seeking Help** section to close the lesson. This is a reminder for you to invite God into your spiritual-growth process. If you choose to write out a prayer in this section, come back to it as you work through the lesson and continue to seek the Holy Spirit's guidance as you discover God's will for your life.

Tips for Small Groups

A small group is a dynamic thing. One week it might seem like a group of close-knit friends. The next it might seem more like a group of uncomfortable strangers. A small-group leader's role is to read these subtle changes and adjust the tone of the discussion accordingly.

Small groups need to be safe places for people to talk openly. It is through shared wrestling with difficult life issues that some of the greatest personal growth is discovered. But in order for the group to feel safe, participants need to know it's okay *not* to share sometimes. Always invite honest disclosure, but never force someone to speak if he or she isn't comfortable doing so. (A savvy leader will follow up later with a group member who isn't comfortable sharing in a group setting to see if a one-on-one discussion is more appropriate.)

Have volunteers take turns reading excerpts from Scripture or from the commentary. The more each person is involved even in the mundane tasks, the more they'll feel comfortable opening up in more meaningful ways.

The leader should watch the clock and keep the discussion moving. Sometimes there may be more Going Deeper questions than your group can cover in your available time. If you've had a fruitful discussion, it's okay to move on without finishing everything. And if you think the group is getting bogged down on a question or has taken off on a tangent, you can simply say, "Let's go on to question 5." Be sure to save at least ten to fifteen minutes for the Going Forward questions.

Finally, soak your group meetings in prayer—before you begin, during as needed, and always at the end of your time together.

Bad News, Good News
(GALATIANS 1:1–10)

Before you begin ...
- *Pray for the Holy Spirit to reveal truth and wisdom as you go through this lesson.*
- *Read Galatians 1:1–10. This lesson references chapter 1 in* Be Free. *It will be helpful for you to have your Bible and a copy of the commentary available as you work through this lesson.*

Getting Started

From the Commentary

The lad at my front door was trying to sell me a subscription to a weekly newspaper, and he was very persuasive. "It only costs a quarter a week," he said, "and the best thing about this newspaper is that it prints only the good news!"

In a world filled with trouble, it is becoming more and more difficult to find any "good news," so perhaps the newspaper was a bargain after all. To the person who has trusted Christ as Savior, the real "good news" is the gospel: "Christ died for our sins according to the scriptures ... he was buried, and ... he rose again the third day according to the scriptures" (1 Cor. 15:3–4). It is the good news that sinners can be forgiven and go to heaven because of what Jesus Christ did on the cross. The good news of salvation through faith in Christ is the most important message in the world.

—*Be Free,* page 19

1. Why do you think Paul introduces this letter as he does? What can we tell from this introduction about the possible problems the Galatian churches are facing? Why is it important for Paul to establish that he is not sent "by man, but by Jesus Christ and God the Father"?

More to Consider: As with many of Paul's letters, Galatians was written to combat specific problems in the early church. Paul himself likely had visited Galatia (in modern-day Turkey) early in his ministry. As you read through this first chapter of Galatians, what can you tell about Paul's previous relationship with this church (or these "churches," as it is noted in Galatians 1:2)?

2. Choose one verse or phrase from Galatians 1:1–10 that stands out to you. This could be something you're intrigued by, something that makes you uncomfortable, something that puzzles you, something that resonates with you, or just something you want to examine further. Write that here.

Going Deeper

From the Commentary

> [At the outset of Galatians, Paul] is careful to let the [Galatian Christians] know the authority he has from the Lord. He has three sources of authority.
>
> *(1) His ministry* (1:1–2). In the early days of the church, God called special men to do special tasks. Among them were the *apostles*. The word means "one who is sent with a commission." … Paul himself was neither a disciple nor an apostle during Christ's earthly ministry, but he had seen the risen Lord and been commissioned by Him (Acts 9:1–18; 1 Cor. 9:1).
>
> *(2) His message* (1:3–4). From the very beginning, Paul clearly stated the message of the gospel because it was this message that the Judaizers were changing.

(3) His motive (1:5). The false teachers were not ministering for the glory of Christ, but for their own glory (see Gal. 6:12–14).… But Paul's motive was pure and godly: He wanted to glorify Jesus Christ (see 1 Cor. 6:19–20; 10:31–33).

—*Be Free*, pages 20, 22

3. Why do you think Paul opens his letter by describing his qualifications for presenting the message? What objection does each of the sources of authority (as noted by Wiersbe in the previous excerpt) answer? What does this letter tell you about challenges facing the early church? How are these like or unlike the challenges the church faces today?

More to Consider: The term Judaizers *refers to leaders who teach that it is necessary for Christians both to have faith in Christ and to adhere to the law of Moses, a requirement for followers of Judaism. What would have made it tempting for young Christian believers to follow the line of thinking presented by Judaizers?*

From the Commentary

"I am amazed that you are so quickly moving away!" This was the first reason for Paul's anxiety: The Galatians were *deserting the grace of God.* (The verb indicates they were in the process of deserting and had not fully turned away.)

Paul struck while the iron was hot. God had called them in His grace and saved them from their sins. Now they were moving from grace back into law. They were abandoning liberty for legalism! And they were doing it so quickly, without consulting Paul, their "spiritual father," or giving time for the Holy Spirit to teach them.

—*Be Free,* page 23

4. Why is it "really no gospel at all" (Gal. 1:7) to believe one needs Christ plus something else (in this case, the law of Moses) in order to please God? Why does Paul offer such strong language to challenge this perversion of the true gospel? How does Paul communicate his urgency through this letter?

From Today's World

Legalism is alive and well in many modern Christian churches, though it takes on a different look than what Paul saw in the Galatian church. Whether stated outright as a requirement for acceptance by God or (more commonly) implied by way of requirement before becoming a church member or full insider, churches today continue to fail the test of what Paul calls the "gospel of grace." Some churches might press people to embrace Christ-plus-our-political-views. Or Christ-plus-these-acts-of-service. In each of these cases, the fact that churches are adding to the gospel suggests they are much like the Judaizers.

5. What are some of the things churches add to the gospel today? What are the good intentions behind those additions? What makes them similar to the requirements of the Judaizers in Paul's day?

From the Commentary

"The grace of God" is a basic theme in this letter (Gal. 1:3, 6, 15; 2:9, 21; 5:4; 6:18). Grace is simply God's favor to undeserving sinners. The words *grace* and *gift* go together, because salvation is the gift of God through His grace (Eph. 2:8–10). The Galatian believers were not simply "changing religions" or "changing churches" but were actually abandoning the very grace of God! To make matters worse, they were deserting the very God of grace! God had called them and saved them; now they were deserting Him for human leaders who would bring them into bondage.

—*Be Free*, page 23

6. Why might the Galatian Christians abandon grace in favor of a set of rules or laws? What makes a system of laws compelling to those seeking favor with God?

From the Commentary

[The Galatians] were guilty of another sin that gave Paul great anxiety: *They were perverting the gospel of God.* The Judaizers claimed to be preaching "the gospel," but there cannot be two gospels, one centered in works and the other centered in grace. "They are not preaching another gospel," wrote Paul, "but a *different* message—one so different from the true gospel that it is no gospel at all." Like the cultists today, the Judaizers would say,

"We believe in Jesus Christ—*but* we have something wonderful *to add* to what you already believe."

—*Be Free*, pages 23–24

7. The Judaizers wanted to add Jewish cultural customs (such as food taboos) to their version of the gospel. What are some cultural customs among American Christians that are good in themselves but not gospel requirements?

From the Commentary

"Make love, not war!" may have been a popular slogan, but it is not always feasible. Doctors must make war against disease and death; sanitary engineers must war against filth and pollution; legislators must war against injustice and crime. And they all fight *because of something they love!*

"Ye that love the LORD, hate evil" (Ps. 97:10). "Abhor that which is evil; cleave to that which is good" (Rom. 12:9). Paul waged war against the false teachers because he loved the truth and because he loved those whom he had led to Christ. Like a loving father who guards his daughter until

she is married, Paul watched over his converts lest they be
seduced into sin (2 Cor. 11:1–4).

—*Be Free*, page 25

8. Review Galatians 1:6–9. What is the "war" that Paul is waging in these
verses? According to Paul, how do we know which teachers are "false
teachers"? What is prompting such strong language from Paul? Do you see
the same kind of passion in today's church? Explain.

*More to Consider: The word translated "pervert" in verse 7 is also
used in Acts 13:10. It means "to turn about" or "to reverse." Why do
you think Paul uses the word in each of these contexts?*

From the Commentary

When Verdi produced his first opera in Florence, the
composer stood by himself in the shadows and kept his
eye on the face of one man in the audience—the great
Rossini. It mattered not to Verdi whether the people in the

hall were cheering him or jeering him; all he wanted was a smile of approval from the master musician. So it was with Paul. He knew what it was to suffer for the gospel, but the approval or disapproval of men did not move him.

—*Be Free*, pages 26–27

9. Circle Galatians 1:10. Why do you think Paul included this in his letter? What specific concerns might he be addressing? What are the signs that tell us someone is trying to win the approval of men and not God?

From the Commentary

We have noted three steps Paul took toward engaging these false teachers in battle: He explained his authority, expressed his anxiety, and exposed his adversaries. But how was he going to attack his enemies? What approach would he use to convince the Galatian believers that all they needed was faith in God's grace? A quick survey of the entire letter shows that Paul was a master defender of the gospel. Take time to read the entire letter at one sitting, and as you read, note the three approaches that Paul took.

His first approach was *personal* (Gal. 1—2).

Galatians 3 and 4 are *doctrinal*.

The final two chapters of the letter are *practical*.

—*Be Free*, pages 27–28

10. Paul sometimes comes off as sounding self-important in his letters, as in Galatians 1:1, 8, 10 (see also 1:13–24). What gives this impression? Why do you think Paul felt compelled to speak so confidently of his role in the early church? What did this say about Paul? About the manner in which God used Paul?

Looking Inward

Take a moment to reflect on all that you've explored thus far in this study of Galatians 1:1–10. Review your notes and answers and think about how each of these things matters in your life today.

Tips for Small Groups: To get the most out of this section, form pairs or trios and have group members take turns answering these questions. Be honest and as open as you can in this discussion, but most of all, be encouraging and supportive of others. Be sensitive to those who are going through particularly difficult times and don't press people to speak if they're uncomfortable doing so.

11. Paul doesn't hold anything back in Galatians 1 when describing his role in the church. What do you see as your role? How confident are you in that role? What is the line between confidence and bragging?

12. Have you ever deserted the gospel of grace Paul is referring to in this letter? If so, what did that look like? What was it that tempted you away from the gospel of grace? What did you do to rediscover grace?

13. In what ways do you feel "called by God"? When did you first hear this calling? How has it changed as you have grown in your faith?

Going Forward

14. Think of one or two things that you have learned that you'd like to work on in the coming week. Remember that this is all about quality, not quantity. It's better to work on one specific area of life and do it well than to work on many and do poorly (or to be so overwhelmed that you simply don't try).

Do you need to be clearer on the difference between the gospel and cultural customs? Do you need to listen more closely to God's call on your life? Be specific. Go back through Galatians 1:1–10 and put a star next to the phrase or verse that is most challenging to you. Consider memorizing this verse.

Real-Life Application Ideas: Review the basic tenets of faith that your church holds to, checking each of them against Scripture to discover their origins. Then consider the things you believe that aren't explicitly covered in those tenets. How does each of them hold up in light of Scripture? If you discover any beliefs that might be considered "added on" to the gospel of grace, talk with a trusted friend or your pastor about them.

Seeking Help

15. Write a prayer below (or simply pray one in silence), inviting God to work on your mind and heart in those areas you've previously noted. Be honest about your desires and fears.

Notes for Small Groups:

- *Look for ways to put into practice the things you wrote in the Going Forward section. Talk with other group members about your ideas and commit to being accountable to one another.*
- *During the coming week, ask the Holy Spirit to continue to reveal truth to you from what you've read and studied.*
- *Before you start the next lesson, read Galatians 1:11–24. For more in-depth lesson preparation, read chapter 2, "Born Free!" in Be Free.*

Born Free

(GALATIANS 1:11–24)

Before you begin …
- *Pray for the Holy Spirit to reveal truth and wisdom as you go through this lesson.*
- *Read Galatians 1:11–24. This lesson references chapter 2 in* Be Free. *It will be helpful for you to have your Bible and a copy of the commentary available as you work through this lesson.*

Getting Started

From the Commentary

Paul's enemies pointed to his nonconformity as proof that his message and ministry were not really of God. "He claims to be an apostle," they argued, "but he does not stand in the apostolic tradition." It is this misrepresentation that Paul answered in this section of Galatians. His nonconformity was divinely deliberate. God had chosen to reveal Himself in a different way to Paul.

—*Be Free,* page 31

1. Why do you think the Galatian Christians were so quick to challenge Paul's authority? What sorts of discussions might have been swirling around the Galatian church that might have promoted this line of thinking? In what ways might this be like the tendency to pass rumors along that exists in today's church?

More to Consider: Read Acts 22 and 26. What do these chapters teach us about Paul's past conduct as an unconverted Jewish rabbi? What is significant about this in light of Paul's arguments in Galatians 1:13–14?

2. Choose one verse or phrase from Galatians 1:11–24 that stands out to you. This could be something you're intrigued by, something that makes you uncomfortable, something that puzzles you, something that resonates with you, or just something you want to examine further. Write that here.

Going Deeper

From the Commentary

> Paul actually thought that Jesus was an impostor and
> His message of salvation a lie. He was sure that God had
> spoken through Moses, but how could he be sure that God
> had spoken through Jesus of Nazareth? Steeped in Jewish
> tradition, young Saul of Tarsus championed his faith.
> His reputation as a zealous persecutor of "the sect of the
> Nazarenes" became known far and wide (see Acts 9:13–14).
>
> —*Be Free*, page 33

3. Read Acts 9:13–14, which describes Paul's previous reputation as a persecutor of Christ-followers. How does this reputation play into his arguments in Galatians 1? What are some clues in Galatians 1:11–24 that point to the resistance Paul was facing from the Galatian Christians?

From the Commentary

> No matter how you look at it, the conversion of Paul was
> a spiritual miracle. It was humanly impossible for Rabbi

Saul to become the apostle Paul apart from the miracle of God's grace. And the same God who saved Paul also called him to be an apostle and gave him the message of the gospel. *For the Judaizers to deny Paul's apostleship and gospel was the same as denying his conversion!*

—*Be Free*, pages 33–34

4. In what ways do you see Paul's conversion as a miracle? Why is that important for Paul's converts to understand? What does Paul's miraculous turnaround tell us about how God sometimes works in the lives of nonbelievers? What are some examples of similar "life change" miracles you've heard about or witnessed in today's church?

From the History Books

One of the greatest appeals of any religious movement is the promise of "life change." To people who are struggling emotionally, relationally, or financially, the idea that something as simple as following a new belief system can turn their circumstance around can be awfully compelling. This is not only the draw of traditional churches, though, it is also the promise offered by cults and questionably motivated organizations. Throughout history, people have been drawn to these groups by a promise of a "better life" or a "more fulfilling" life, only to be drawn into practices that range from mildly heretical to seriously dangerous.

5. How is the draw of Christianity different than that of cults and nonorthodox religious movements? How is it similar? What is the difference between making a true commitment of faith and falling for a belief system that is not the gospel of grace Paul preaches?

More to Consider: Read Galatians 1:15–16, 24. Describe the characteristics of Paul's conversion, as Paul himself explains it in these verses.

From the Commentary

God chose Paul, not only to save him but also to use him to win others. In the Bible, the doctrine of election is never taught with a view to producing pride or selfishness. Election involves responsibility. God chose Paul to preach among the Gentiles the same grace that he had experienced.

—*Be Free*, page 35

6. How is Paul's decision to preach the gospel of grace to the Gentiles evidence that Paul's conversion is of God? What might cause the Galatian Christians to question his conversion? What does this tell you about the influence of Judaizers in the Galatian church?

From the Commentary

> Our Lord's ministry was to the nation of Israel, and so was the ministry of the apostles for the first few years (see Acts 1—7). The death of Stephen was a turning point. As the believers were scattered, they took the good news with them to other places (Acts 8:4; 11:19ff.).
>
> —*Be Free*, pages 36–37

7. Read Acts 7—8. In what ways was Stephen's death a turning point in the Lord's ministry? How do you think Paul looked back on that event? In what ways might that have shaped his approach to ministry after his conversion? In what ways was Paul's personality much the same before and after his conversion? (See Gal. 1:13–14.) How did God use Paul "as he was" to accomplish His plan?

From the Commentary

> Paul gave himself to study, prayer, and meditation, and met with the Lord alone. He may have spent the greater part of three years in Arabia (Gal. 1:17–18), and no doubt was involved in evangelism as well as personal spiritual growth. The apostles had received three years of teaching from the Lord Jesus, and now Paul was going to have his own opportunity to be taught of the Lord.
>
> —*Be Free*, page 37

8. Why is it important to note the time Paul spent in study? What does this say about the importance of study for church leaders today? What are the risks or dangers of putting someone in a leadership position before he or she is well trained?

More to Consider: Paul didn't visit Jerusalem right after his three years of study and prayer and meditation, though this would have seemed logical. Why do you think God directed Paul to go back to Damascus (1:17)?

From the Commentary

In the light of Paul's conduct, his conversion, and his contacts, how could anybody accuse him of borrowing or inventing either his message or his ministry? Certainly he *did* receive his gospel by a revelation from Jesus Christ. Therefore, we must be careful what we do with this gospel, for it is not the invention of men, but the very truth of God.

Some critical scholars have accused Paul of "corrupting the simple gospel," but the evidence is against this accusation. *The same Christ who taught on earth also taught through Paul from heaven.*

—*Be Free*, pages 38–39

9. Read Galatians 1:11–12, 15–17. What do these verses tell us about Paul? Why is it significant that Paul mentions he was "set apart from birth" by God? What does this tell us about the way God chooses whom He uses to preach and teach the gospel?

From the Commentary

> Modern-day "Judaizers," like their ancient counterparts, reject the authority of Paul and try to undermine the gospel that he preached. In Paul's day, their message was "the gospel *plus* Moses." In our day it is "the gospel *plus*" any number of religious leaders, religious books, or religious organizations. "You cannot be saved unless ..." is their message (Acts 15:1), and that "unless" usually includes joining their group and obeying their rules.
>
> —*Be Free*, page 39

10. Who are the modern-day Judaizers? What aspects of Paul's teaching do these Christ-plus-something-else people tend to attack? What are the "unless ..." actions that today's church must confront in order to be true to the gospel?

Looking Inward

Take a moment to reflect on all that you've explored thus far in this study of Galatians 1:11–24. Review your notes and answers and think about how each of these things matters in your life today.

Tips for Small Groups: To get the most out of this section, form pairs or trios and have group members take turns answering these questions. Be honest and as open as you can in this discussion, but most of all, be encouraging and supportive of others. Be sensitive to those who are going through particularly difficult times and don't press people to speak if they're uncomfortable doing so.

11. Recall the time you came to faith in Christ. If this happened in adult life, how do you see yourself as different today than before your conversion? What evidence would friends and family have that your conversion was true?

12. The stoning of Stephen was a turning point in the early church. What are the "turning points" in your own faith story? How did God use those events or moments to direct your path? What sacrifices were made to turn you toward God?

13. What are some of the "unless you ..." additions to the gospel you've struggled with? What makes these beliefs or actions so tempting to you? What would it take for you to let go of these things and fully embrace the gospel of grace?

Going Forward

14. Think of one or two things that you have learned that you'd like to work on in the coming week. Remember that this is all about quality, not quantity. It's better to work on one specific area of life and do it well than to work on many and do poorly (or to be so overwhelmed that you simply don't try).

Do you need to reconsider the things you might be adding on to the gospel? Do you need to ask God for guidance as you seek understanding about unfamiliar doctrines? Be specific. Go back through Galatians 1:11–24 and put a star next to the phrase or verse that is most encouraging to you. Consider memorizing this verse.

Real-Life Application Ideas: Interview a half dozen or more people in your church about their conversion stories. Note whether they came to Christ suddenly or gradually, as adults or beginning when they were children. Do their stories have the "before" and "after" elements that Paul's has? As you listen to these stories, look for clues that tell you more about how God goes about His greater plan of bringing glory to Himself.

Seeking Help

15. Write a prayer below (or simply pray one in silence), inviting God to work on your mind and heart in those areas you've previously noted. Be honest about your desires and fears.

Notes for Small Groups:

- *Look for ways to put into practice the things you wrote in the Going Forward section. Talk with other group members about your ideas and commit to being accountable to one another.*

- *During the coming week, ask the Holy Spirit to continue to reveal truth to you from what you've read and studied.*

- *Before you start the next lesson, read Galatians 2. For more in-depth lesson preparation, read chapters 3 and 4, "The Freedom Fighter—Part 1" and "The Freedom Fighter—Part 2," in* Be Free.

Freedom Fighter
(GALATIANS 2)

Before you begin ...
- *Pray for the Holy Spirit to reveal truth and wisdom as you go through this lesson.*
- *Read Galatians 2. This lesson references chapters 3 and 4 in* Be Free. *It will be helpful for you to have your Bible and a copy of the commentary available as you work through this lesson.*

Getting Started

From the Commentary

Paul's first fight for Christian liberty was at the Jerusalem Council (Acts 15:1–35; Gal. 2:1–10); his second was at a private meeting with Peter (Gal. 2:11–21). Had Paul been unwilling to wage this spiritual warfare, the church in the first century might have become only a Jewish sect, preaching a mixture of law and grace. But because of

Paul's courage, the gospel was kept free from legalism, and it was carried to the Gentiles with great blessing.

—*Be Free,* page 43

1. What are some of the things you discover about Paul from Galatians 2:1–10? What challenges did he face in Jerusalem? What tactics does he use when confronting Peter in Galatians 2:11–21?

More to Consider: Barnabas was an early Christian convert who, like Paul, came from Jewish heritage. Along with Paul, Barnabas focused his efforts in defending Gentile converts against the Judaizers. Why do you think Paul and Barnabas were called to speak to the Gentiles instead of the Jewish Christians? What unique gifts or experiences might they have had that gave them credibility with these new believers?

2. Choose one verse or phrase from Galatians 2 that stands out to you. This could be something you're intrigued by, something that makes you uncomfortable, something that puzzles you, something that resonates with you, or just something you want to examine further. Write that here.

Going Deeper

From the Commentary

> Paul and Barnabas had returned to Antioch from their
> first missionary journey, excited about the way God had
> "opened the door of faith unto the Gentiles" (Acts 14:27).
> But the Jewish legalists in Jerusalem were upset with their
> report; so they came to Antioch and taught, in effect, that
> a Gentile had to become a Jew before he could become a
> Christian (15:1).
>
> —*Be Free*, page 45

3. What were the results of the private consultation noted in Galatians
2:1–10? How was it significant that Peter, James, and John (all circumcised
Jewish Christians) didn't ask Titus to be circumcised according to
the Jewish law?

From the Commentary

> Ever since Paul's time, the enemies of grace have been
> trying to add something to the simple gospel of the grace

of God. They tell us that a man is saved by faith in Christ *plus* something—good works, the Ten Commandments, baptism, church membership, religious ritual—and Paul made it clear that these teachers are wrong. In fact, Paul pronounced a curse on any person (man or angel) who preaches any other gospel than the gospel of the grace of God, centered in Jesus Christ (Gal 1:6–9; see 1 Cor. 15:1–7 for a definition of the gospel). It is a serious thing to tamper with the gospel.

—*Be Free*, page 49

4. What is Paul referring to when he describes how "false brothers had infiltrated our ranks to spy on the freedom we have in Christ Jesus and to make us slaves" (Gal. 2:4)? What did they want, and how would giving them what they wanted have made Paul and his companions slaves?

From the History Books

The Council of Jerusalem occurred sometime around AD 50 and apparently was to resolve a disagreement that began in Antioch regarding the need for believers to be circumcised. The debate was between Paul and those who believed that Gentile converts needed to live like Jewish Christians in order to be fully Christian. As with other important councils in the days of the early church, the goal was to come away with an agreement on the contentious issues so that the church might grow more efficiently and according to the same, agreed-upon doctrine.

5. Why do you think the question of Gentiles becoming Jewish required a council as opposed to simply one-on-one meetings between Paul and those who espoused a different belief? Why does Paul make a point in this letter to the Galatians that his efforts were met with agreement? (See Gal. 2:2–3, 9.)

From the Commentary

> Not only did the assembly approve Paul's gospel and oppose Paul's enemies, but they also encouraged Paul's ministry and recognized publicly that God had committed the Gentile aspect of His work into Paul's hands. They could add nothing to Paul's message or ministry, and they dared not take anything away. There was agreement and unity: One gospel would be preached to Jews and to Gentiles.

However, the leaders recognized that God had assigned different areas of ministry to different men.

—Be Free, page 49

6. Why do you think God chose Paul to reach out to the Gentiles with the gospel? What, if anything, about the choice of Paul seems surprising to you? What in Paul's own story would have prepared him well to speak to the Gentiles?

From the Commentary

Even though the conference ended with Paul and the leaders in agreement, it did not permanently solve the problem. The Judaizers did not give up, but persisted in interfering with Paul's work and invading the churches he founded. Paul carried the good news of the council's decision to the churches in Antioch, Syria, and Cilicia (Acts 15:23) and in the other areas where he had ministered (16:4). But the Judaizers followed at his heels (like yelping dogs, see Phil. 3:1–3), starting at Antioch where they even swayed Peter to their cause (see Gal. 2:11ff.).

—Be Free, page 51

7. How is the book of Galatians itself evidence that the Council of Jerusalem didn't solve the problem at hand? Why do you suppose some Jewish Christians (the Judaizers) found it so hard to accept that God no longer required His people to keep the law He had given to Moses? What prompts people today to become antagonistic toward those who preach the gospel of grace?

From the Commentary

Apparently, sometime after the important conference described in Acts 15, Peter came from Jerusalem to Antioch. The first thing to note is *Peter's freedom* then. He enjoyed fellowship with *all* the believers, Jews and Gentiles alike. To "eat with the Gentiles" meant to accept them, to put Jews and Gentiles on the same level as one family in Christ.

Raised as an orthodox Jew, Peter had a difficult time learning this lesson. Jesus had taught it while He was with Peter before the crucifixion (Matt. 15:1–20). The Holy Spirit had reemphasized it when He sent Peter to the home of Cornelius, the Roman centurion (Acts 10). Furthermore, the truth had been accepted and approved by the conference of leaders at Jerusalem (Acts 15). Peter had been one of the key witnesses at that time.

Peter's freedom was threatened by *Peter's fear*.

How do we account for this fear? For one thing, we know that Peter was an impulsive man. He could show amazing faith and courage one minute and fail completely the next.

—*Be Free*, pages 55–56

8. What makes Peter's fall so tragic? How are his fears like or unlike those faced by well-meaning Christians today? Why do you think Paul confronts Peter in front of the other Christians (Gal. 2:14)? What is the point of this challenge to Peter? How do the verses that follow support Paul's challenge?

More to Consider: How might Paul's words in 2:14–21 have been viewed as controversial by Jewish Christians who had kept the Jewish law since they were children? Why would they feel that way?

From the Commentary

There are five basic Christian doctrines that were being denied by Peter because of his separation from the Gentiles.

(1) The unity of the church (Gal. 2:14).

(2) Justification by faith (vv. 15–16).

(3) Freedom from the law (vv. 17–18).

(4) The very gospel itself (vv. 19–20).

(5) The grace of God (v. 21).

—*Be Free*, pages 57–60

9. Consider each of the doctrines Paul addresses as outlined in the commentary excerpt you just read. What does each doctrine mean? How does each one speak to Peter's errors? In what ways are these doctrines at issue in today's church?

From the Commentary

> We have no record of Peter's reply to Paul's rebuke, but
> Scripture would indicate that he admitted his sin and
> was restored to the fellowship once again. Certainly
> when you read his two letters (1 and 2 Peter) you detect
> no deviation from the gospel of the grace of God. In fact,
> the theme of 1 Peter is "the true grace of God" (1 Peter
> 5:12); and the word *grace* is used in every chapter of the
> letter. Peter is careful to point out that he and Paul were
> in complete agreement, lest anyone try to "rob Peter to
> pay Paul" (2 Peter 3:15–16).
>
> —*Be Free*, page 61

10. Is it important to the Christian faith that Peter acknowledged the grace of God? Why or why not? What does Peter's story teach us about the very grace Paul preaches?

Looking Inward

Take a moment to reflect on all that you've explored thus far in this study of Galatians 2. Review your notes and answers and think about how each of these things matters in your life today.

Tips for Small Groups: To get the most out of this section, form pairs or trios and have group members take turns answering these questions. Be honest and as open as you can in this discussion, but most of all, be encouraging and supportive of others. Be sensitive to those who are going through particularly difficult times and don't press people to speak if they're uncomfortable doing so.

11. Have you ever been put on the spot for your beliefs (either within or outside of church walls)? If so, how did you respond? What evidences did you give to support your perspective? Did you end up changing your views? Why or why not? How did that circumstance affect your relationship with other church members?

12. Paul writes in Galatians 2:6, "God does not judge by external appearance." When have you judged others by their appearance or apparent actions? Were you right? Wrong? What did you learn about them? About yourself?

13. How might you have felt if you were being confronted by Paul over a theological issue? What would your initial reaction have been to the accusation that you were "clearly in the wrong"? Based on what you know from Paul's interaction with Peter, what is a biblical response to this sort of circumstance? What can this teach you about responding to conflict or controversy?

Going Forward

14. Think of one or two things that you have learned that you'd like to work on in the coming week. Remember that this is all about quality, not quantity. It's better to work on one specific area of life and do it well than to work on many and do poorly (or to be so overwhelmed that you simply don't try).

Do you need to brush up on your doctrine so you can answer challenges to it? Be specific. Go back through Galatians 2 and put a star next to the phrase or verse that is most encouraging to you. Consider memorizing this verse.

Real-Life Application Ideas: Take a close look at the practices and doctrines of your church or small group. Talk with other members to uncover any areas of question or concern, then invite your church leaders to lead a class specifically addressing those questions and concerns. Use this time for healthy dialogue and to celebrate unity in the things that matter and diversity in those that don't.

Seeking Help

15. Write a prayer below (or simply pray one in silence), inviting God to work on your mind and heart in those areas you've previously noted. Be honest about your desires and fears.

Notes for Small Groups:

- *Look for ways to put into practice the things you wrote in the Going Forward section. Talk with other group members about your ideas and commit to being accountable to one another.*

- *During the coming week, ask the Holy Spirit to continue to reveal truth to you from what you've read and studied.*

- *Before you start the next lesson, read Galatians 3. For more in-depth lesson preparation, read chapters 5 and 6, "Bewitched and Bothered" and "The Logic of Law," in* Be Free.

The Law
(GALATIANS 3)

Before you begin …
- *Pray for the Holy Spirit to reveal truth and wisdom as you go through this lesson.*
- *Read Galatians 3. This lesson references chapters 5 and 6 in* Be Free. *It will be helpful for you to have your Bible and a copy of the commentary available as you work through this lesson.*

Getting Started

From the Commentary

Paul used six different arguments to prove that God saves sinners through faith in Christ and not by the works of the law. He began with the *personal argument* (Gal. 3:1–5), in which he asked the Galatians to recall their personal experience with Christ when they were saved. Then he moved into the *scriptural argument* (vv. 6–14), in which he quoted six Old Testament passages to prove his point. In the *logical argument* (vv. 15–29) he reasoned with his readers on the basis of what a covenant is and how a covenant works. He then presented the *historical argument* (Gal. 4:1–11), explaining the place of law in the history of Israel.

At this point, Paul's love for his converts came to the surface. The result is a *sentimental argument* (Gal. 4:12–18) as the apostle appealed to them to remember his love and their happy relationship in days past. But then Paul went right back to his close reasoning, and concluded with the *allegorical argument* (vv. 19–31) based on the life of Abraham and his relationships with Sarah and Hagar.

—*Be Free,* pages 67–68

1. Why do you think Paul uses so many different arguments to prove his point? Go through Galatians 3 and identify the first three arguments. What sort of audience might each of these arguments speak to most directly?

2. Choose one verse or phrase from Galatians 3 that stands out to you. This could be something you're intrigued by, something that makes you uncomfortable, something that puzzles you, something that resonates with you, or just something you want to examine further. Write that here.

Going Deeper

From the Commentary

> The key to [the personal argument] is in the word *suffered* (Gal. 3:4), which can be translated "experienced." Paul asked, "Have you experienced so many things in vain?" The argument from Christian experience was a wise one with which to begin, because Paul had been with them when they had trusted Christ.
>
> —*Be Free*, page 68

3. What is Paul's personal argument for grace in 3:1–5? What are the strengths of this argument? What are the dangers of arguing from experience? How can Christians effectively avoid those dangers while still utilizing their own experience to share the gospel of grace?

More to Consider: What questions does Paul ask in 3:1–5? What issue does each of these questions address in his argument for God's grace?

From the Commentary

> We never judge the Scriptures by our experience; we test
> our experience by the Word of God. In [Galatians 3:1–5],
> Paul asked six questions; in [3:6–14] he will quote six
> Old Testament statements to prove that salvation is by
> faith in Christ and not by the works of the law. Since the
> Judaizers wanted to take the believers back into the law,
> Paul quoted the law! And since they magnified the place
> of Abraham in their religion, Paul used Abraham as one
> of his witnesses!
>
> —*Be Free*, page 71

4. Read Genesis 12:1–5 (which Paul quotes). How was Abraham a good example of a man who lived his life by faith in God? Where do you see in God's words here the promise that salvation would be for Gentiles too and not just for those who keep the Jewish law? Why is it important for Paul to show that his understanding of the gospel is rooted in the Scriptures, not just in personal experience?

From Today's World

Today's churches are as varied as ever, both in their "look" and in the way they deliver the gospel message. Some only use Scripture to teach and preach while others incorporate other resources into the message and ministry. Some are all about evangelism while others are all about social action. This diversity means there is a "church for everyone"—from the person longing to experience the presence of God in a free-flowing service to the person who prefers to sit in silence and reflect on God's Word as interpreted from the pulpit.

5. What does the diversity of churches tell us about the gospel? About those who seek to know God? What happens to a church when it relegates "experience" as meaningless to the maturing process? What happens to a church when it relies too much on experience and not enough on Scripture?

From the Commentary

Salvation could never come by obedience to law because the law brings a curse, not a blessing. [In 3:10–12,] Paul quoted from Deuteronomy 27:26. Law demands obedience, and this means obedience in *all things*. The law is not a "religious cafeteria" where people can pick and choose (see James 2:10–11).

—*Be Free*, page 73

6. In what ways do Christians today see Scripture as a "spiritual cafeteria"? How might Paul speak to those who pick and choose what to follow or believe?

More to Consider: The word redeemed *in 3:13 means to purchase a slave for the purpose of setting him free. It was, of course, typical for people in Paul's day to purchase a slave and keep him as a slave. Why would this imagery be particularly relevant to Paul's discourse on the role of "law" for those who trust Christ?*

From the Commentary

Instead of worshipping God "in spirit and in truth" (John 4:24), the legalist invents his own system that satisfies his senses. He cannot walk by faith; he has to walk by sight and hearing and tasting and smelling and feeling. To be sure, true Spirit-led worship does not deny the five senses. We see other believers; we sing and hear the hymns; we taste and feel the elements of the Lord's Supper. But these external things are but windows through which faith perceives the eternal.

—*Be Free*, page 75

7. In what ways might living by the Jewish law instead of by faith and the Holy Spirit's guidance (3:3–5) have seemed easier to the Galatians? In what ways does it sometimes seem easier today to live by the rules of a religious subculture rather than by faith in Christ and through the Holy Spirit? What are some of the "external things" that are so easy to latch onto today?

From the Commentary

The Judaizers had Paul in a corner. He had just finished proving from the Old Testament that God's plan of salvation left no room for the works of the law. But the fact that Paul quoted six times from the Old Testament raised a serious problem: If salvation does not involve the law, then why was the law given in the first place? Paul quoted from the law to prove the insignificance of the law. If the law is now set aside, then his very arguments are worthless, because they are taken from the law.

—*Be Free*, page 79

8. Review Galatians 3:15–20. How does Paul compare the law (given to Moses) with the promises of God (given 430 years earlier to Abraham)? Why is this distinction important to his argument against his opponents who want all Christians to live by the Jewish law?

From the Commentary

You can almost hear the Judaizers shouting the question in Galatians 3:21: "Is the law then *against* the promises of God?" Is God contradicting Himself? Does His right hand not know what His left hand is doing? As he replied to this question, Paul revealed his deep insight into the ways and purposes of God.

—*Be Free*, page 83

9. Read Galatians 3:21–29. How does Paul answer the Judaizers' questions? What is the relationship between God's law and God's grace/promise? In what ways were the Jews (before Christ) "held prisoner by the law"? How did the law lead us to Christ?

From the Commentary

> With the coming of Jesus Christ, the nation of Israel moved out of childhood into adulthood. The long period of preparation was over. While there was a certain amount of glory to the law, there was a greater glory in the gracious salvation of God as found in Christ. The law could reveal sin and to a certain extent, control behavior, but the law could not do for the sinner what Jesus Christ can do.
>
> —*Be Free*, pages 85–86

10. According to Paul in 3:21, what can't the law do? Why can't it? What does this mean, practically speaking, for those who choose to follow Christ?

Looking Inward

Take a moment to reflect on all that you've explored thus far in this study of Galatians 3. Review your notes and answers and think about how each of these things matters in your life today.

Tips for Small Groups: To get the most out of this section, form pairs or trios and have group members take turns answering these questions. Be honest and as open as you can in this discussion, but most of all, be encouraging and supportive of others. Be sensitive to those who are going through particularly difficult times and don't press people to speak if they're uncomfortable doing so.

11. When have you been tempted to live by the external rules of a religious subculture instead of by the kind of faith and reliance on the Holy Spirit that transforms a person from the inside? What led you to that place of conflict? Why does the law often seem easier to follow than grace?

12. What does it mean in practice for you to live by faith, not by the external rules of a religious subculture that can't impart life (3:21)? What

shifts in thinking does that involve? What actions? What are the challenges of doing that?

13. How does it make you feel to know that God redeemed you through Jesus Christ? How does knowing this impact your understanding of the role of the law in your everyday practice of faith?

Going Forward

14. Think of one or two things that you have learned that you'd like to work on in the coming week. Remember that this is all about quality, not quantity. It's better to work on one specific area of life and do it well than to work on many and do poorly (or to be so overwhelmed that you simply don't try).

Do you need to better understand the relationship between God's promise and God's law? Be specific. Go back through Galatians 3 and put a star next to the phrase or verse that is most encouraging to you. Consider memorizing this verse.

Real-Life Application Ideas: Do a personal Bible study on the story of Abraham, focusing specifically on how both faith and obedience to commands are interwoven in his story. Then revisit Galatians 3 and review what Paul wrote in light of your discoveries. What does this tell you about the importance of the Old Testament writings in shedding light on the New Testament writings and vice versa?

Seeking Help

15. Write a prayer below (or simply pray one in silence), inviting God to work on your mind and heart in those areas you've previously noted. Be honest about your desires and fears.

Notes for Small Groups:

- *Look for ways to put into practice the things you wrote in the Going Forward section. Talk with other group members about your ideas and commit to being accountable to one another.*

- *During the coming week, ask the Holy Spirit to continue to reveal truth to you from what you've read and studied.*

- *Before you start the next lesson, read Galatians 4. For more in-depth lesson preparation, read chapters 7 and 8, "It's Time to Grow Up!" and "Meet Your Mother,"* in Be Free.

Grow Up!
(GALATIANS 4)

Before you begin …
- *Pray for the Holy Spirit to reveal truth and wisdom as you go through this lesson.*
- *Read Galatians 4. This lesson references chapters 7 and 8 in* Be Free. *It will be helpful for you to have your Bible and a copy of the commentary available as you work through this lesson.*

Getting Started

From the Commentary

One of the tragedies of legalism is that it gives the appearance of spiritual maturity when, in reality, it leads the believer back into a "second childhood" of Christian experience. The Galatian Christians, like most believers, wanted to grow and go forward for Christ, but they were going about it in the wrong way. Their experience is not too different from that of Christians today who get involved in various legalistic movements, hoping to become better Christians. Their motives may be right, but their methods are wrong.

This is the truth Paul was trying to get across to his beloved converts in Galatia.

—*Be Free,* page 91

1. From what you've read in Galatians thus far, what clues do you have that the Galatians had good motives in their attempts to understand what it meant to follow Jesus? How is this similar to the way some churches operate today? Who determines what is an appropriate "method" for following Jesus?

2. Choose one verse or phrase from Galatians 4 that stands out to you. This could be something you're intrigued by, something that makes you uncomfortable, something that puzzles you, something that resonates with you, or just something you want to examine further. Write that here.

Going Deeper

From the Commentary

> Among the blessings of the Christian experience is *adoption* (Gal. 4:5; Eph. 1:5). We do not *enter* God's family by adoption the way a homeless child would enter a loving family in our own society. The only way to get into God's family is by *regeneration*, being "born again" (John 3:3).
>
> The New Testament word for *adoption* means "to place as an adult son." It has to do with our *standing* in the family of God: We are not little children but adult sons with all the privileges of sonship.
>
> We *enter* God's family by regeneration, but we *enjoy* God's family by adoption.
>
> —*Be Free*, page 92

3. What does it mean for those under the law to be redeemed (Gal. 4:4–5)? How might Paul's use of the comparison between "slave" and "son" have been received by the Galatian Christians? How is it important to you that we have the Spirit inside us, calling out to God as an adult son calls out to a good Father (4:6–7)?

More to Consider: What does the phrase "the fullness of time" or "the time had fully come" in verse 4 refer to? Why is it important for Paul to mention this? How does this speak to the Gentile Christians? The Jewish converts?

From the Commentary

What really happened when the Galatians turned from grace to law? To begin with, they abandoned liberty for bondage. When they were ignorant sinners, they had served their false gods and had experienced the tragedy of such pagan slavery. But then they had trusted Christ and been delivered from superstition and slavery. Now they were abandoning their liberty in Christ and going back into bondage. They were dropping out of the school of grace and enrolling in the kindergarten of law! They were destroying all the good work the Lord had done in them through Paul's ministry.

—*Be Free*, page 96

4. Paul wrote, "Formerly, when you did not know God, you were slaves to those who by nature are not gods" (Gal. 4:8). What is Paul referring to? Why would anyone abandon liberty for bondage? What are some of the things people choose today in lieu of the liberty offered by the gospel of grace?

From the History Books

Historically speaking, the Roman Empire played an important role in the gospel story. Thanks to the Roman Empire, roads were built to connect city to city. Roman laws protected the citizens' rights, and soldiers maintained peace throughout the land. Also, because of the Roman conquests (as well as the Greek conquests), both Latin and Greek had become known across the Empire.

5. How did each of the events listed above help prepare the way for the birth of the Savior? What does this say about God's timing? Why might it have been hard for the Judaizers to understand that God had chosen this unique moment in history to do something that would change things so dramatically?

From the Commentary

A true servant of God does not "use people" to build up himself or his work; he ministers in love to help people know Christ better and glorify Him. Beware of that religious worker who wants your exclusive allegiance because he is the only one who is right. He will use you as long as he can and then drop you for somebody else—and your fall will be a painful one. The task of the spiritual leader is to get people to love and follow Christ, not to promote himself and his ministry.

—Be Free, page 99

6. Read Galatians 4:17–18. Why are "those people" zealous to win the Galatian Christians over? What is wrong with their motives? By contrast, what are examples of the good purposes for being zealous that Paul refers to in 4:18?

From the Commentary

Since the Judaizers appealed to the law, Paul accepted their challenge and used the law to prove that Christians are not under the law. He took the familiar story of Ishmael and Isaac (Gen. 16—21) and drew from it basic truths about the Christian's relationship to the law of Moses.

—Be Free, page 103

7. The Judaizers saw themselves as descendants of Abraham; his free wife, Sarah; and their promised son, Isaac. How do you think they might have responded to Paul's argument in 4:21–31 that they were acting like descendants of Abraham's slave woman, Hagar? In what ways are Christians "children of promise" (4:28)? In what ways do we sometimes act like children of the slave woman?

From the Commentary

Paul's use of Genesis in this section does not give us license to find "hidden meanings" in all the events of the Old Testament. If we take that approach to the Bible, we can make it mean almost anything we please. This is the way many false teachings arise. The Holy Spirit inspired Paul to discern the hidden meaning of the Genesis story.

—*Be Free,* page 104

8. In what ways does Paul interpret the Old Testament in light of the new covenant? How is Paul's use of the Old Testament in his argument different from the way many Christians "spiritualize" things in order to give them meaning or value?

More to Consider: Go back through your Bible and study the Old Testament story referenced in 4:21–23. (See Gen. 16; 21:1–12.)

From the Commentary

> We Christians, like Isaac, are the children of promise by grace. The covenant of grace, pictured by Sarah, is our spiritual mother. The law and the old nature (Hagar and Ishmael) want to persecute us and bring us into bondage. How are we to solve this problem?
>
> —*Be Free*, page 109

9. How did Paul answer the problem posed in the excerpt you just read? What does it look like to "cast out the bondwoman (or slave woman) and

her son" in practical terms? Why doesn't the slave woman's son "share in the inheritance with the free woman's son" (Gal. 4:30)?

From the Commentary

> The old nature loves legalism because it gives the old nature a chance to "look good." It costs very little for Ishmael not to do certain bad things, or to do certain religious deeds, just so long as he can remain Ishmael. For seventeen years Ishmael caused no trouble in the home; then Isaac came along, and there was conflict. Legalism caters to Ishmael. The Christian who claims to be spiritual because of what he doesn't do is only fooling himself. It takes more than negations to make a positive, fruitful spiritual life.
>
> —*Be Free*, page 111

10. How does legalism give the old nature a way to "look good"? Why might "looking good" have been so important to the Galatian Christians? How is this still a temptation even today? How does Paul speak directly to this error in Galatians 4?

Looking Inward

Take a moment to reflect on all that you've explored thus far in this study of Galatians 4. Review your notes and answers and think about how each of these things matters in your life today.

Tips for Small Groups: To get the most out of this section, form pairs or trios and have group members take turns answering these questions. Be honest and as open as you can in this discussion, but most of all, be encouraging and supportive of others. Be sensitive to those who are going through particularly difficult times and don't press people to speak if they're uncomfortable doing so.

11. In what ways have you been "in slavery" under the principles of the world? What does it mean to you that you are a son or daughter and no longer a slave? How does that impact the way you live each day?

12. Have you ever been in a similar place to that of the Galatian Christians, whom Paul accuses of having lost their joy (Gal. 4:15)? What prompted those seasons of life? How did you work through them? What are practical ways to rediscover the joy of being a Christ-follower?

13. What is your reaction to Paul's figurative comparison of Abraham's sons? When have you felt like the slave woman's son? Like the free woman's son? If you're feeling more like the slave woman's son, what steps do you need to take to embrace the inheritance offered to those who are free like Isaac?

Going Forward

14. Think of one or two things that you have learned that you'd like to work on in the coming week. Remember that this is all about quality, not quantity. It's better to work on one specific area of life and do it well than to work on many and do poorly (or to be so overwhelmed that you simply don't try).

Do you need to work on accepting the gift of your inheritance through Christ? Do you need to rediscover joy? Be specific. Go back through Galatians 4 and put a star next to the phrase or verse that is most encouraging to you. Consider memorizing this verse.

Real-Life Application Ideas: Come up with a list of things you can do that can engage you (or reengage you) with the life of the local church. This might be something as simple as attending a midweek worship service, or assisting in a Sunday school class. Or it might mean taking on a leadership role or a serving role. As you give yourself to these things, be open to the joy God gives to those who pursue Him zealously.

Seeking Help

15. Write a prayer below (or simply pray one in silence), inviting God to work on your mind and heart in those areas you've previously noted. Be honest about your desires and fears.

Notes for Small Groups:

- *Look for ways to put into practice the things you wrote in the Going Forward section. Talk with other group members about your ideas and commit to being accountable to one another.*

- *During the coming week, ask the Holy Spirit to continue to reveal truth to you from what you've read and studied.*

- *Before you start the next lesson, read Galatians 5:1–12. For more in-depth lesson preparation, read chapter 9, "Stop! Thief!" in* Be Free.

A "Dangerous" Doctrine
(GALATIANS 5:1–12)

Before you begin …
- *Pray for the Holy Spirit to reveal truth and wisdom as you go through this lesson.*
- *Read Galatians 5:1–12. This lesson references chapter 9 in* Be Free. *It will be helpful for you to have your Bible and a copy of the commentary available as you work through this lesson.*

Getting Started

From the Commentary

"Paul's doctrine of grace is dangerous!" cried the Judaizers. "It replaces law with license. Why, if we do away with our rules and abandon our high standards, the churches will fall apart."

Paul turned now from argument to application, from the doctrinal to the practical. The Christian who lives by faith is not going to become a rebel. Quite the contrary, he is going to experience the *inner discipline* of God that is far better than the outer discipline of man-made rules.

—*Be Free,* page 115

1. What does Paul mean by "It is for freedom that Christ has set us free" (Gal. 5:1)? What reason might the Judaizers have given for Christ's sacrifice, if not for freedom? Wiersbe states that the Christian who lives by faith is not going to become a rebel. Why not?

More to Consider: Read Matthew 11:28–30. How is putting on the yoke of Christ an answer to the concern posed in Galatians 5:1? What does it mean to put on the yoke of Christ?

2. Choose one verse or phrase from Galatians 5:1–12 that stands out to you. This could be something you're intrigued by, something that makes you uncomfortable, something that puzzles you, something that resonates with you, or just something you want to examine further. Write that here.

Going Deeper

From the Commentary

> There are some people who feel very insecure with liberty.
> They would rather be under the tyranny of some leader
> than to make their own decisions freely. There are some
> believers who are frightened by the liberty they have
> in God's grace, so they seek out a fellowship that is
> legalistic and dictatorial, where they can let others make
> their decisions for them. This is comparable to an adult
> climbing back into the crib.
>
> —*Be Free*, page 118

3. Paul talks about those who "have fallen away from grace" in Galatians
5:4. Why are some people so uncomfortable with grace and freedom?
What does this tell us about the nature of man? About God's offer of grace?

From the Commentary

> Paul used three phrases to describe the losses the Christian
> incurs when he turns from grace to law: "Christ shall

profit you nothing" (Gal. 5:2); "a debtor to do the whole law" (v. 3); "Christ is become of no effect unto you" (v. 4). This leads to the sad conclusion in Galatians 5:4: "Ye are fallen from grace."

—*Be Free*, page 118

4. Look up Galatians 5:2–6 in a couple different Bible translations. Now rephrase what Paul says about the losses Christians incur when turning to the law instead of grace.

From Today's World

The nightly news is littered with stories of men and women who were on a path to success, only to be tripped up by poor choices or obstacles that they couldn't find a way to circumvent. Many who live under the scrutiny of the public eye find themselves drawn to drugs or alcohol in an attempt to cope with the attention. Athletes take drugs as a shortcut to greater success and instead find themselves no longer able to compete. Businessmen and women are tempted to break the rules for the sake of gain and tumble when their indiscretions become public knowledge.

5. What is it that turns people who are on an essentially good path toward things that knock them off that path? In the case of those who aren't

tripped up, what accounts for the difference? Why are some people able to avoid the temptations and the promise of shortcuts while others are not? What does this teach us about our race for the "prize" that is being made complete in Christ?

From the Commentary

> When we trust Christ, *we become spiritually rich.* We now share in the riches of God's grace (Eph. 1:7), the riches of His glory (v. 18; Phil. 4:19), the riches of His wisdom (Rom. 11:33), and the "unsearchable riches of Christ" (Eph. 3:8). In Christ we have "all the treasures of wisdom and knowledge" (Col. 2:3), and we are "complete in Him" (v. 10).
>
> —*Be Free*, page 119

6. Read the Scripture passages listed in the excerpt you just read. What does each kind of riches mean in practical terms? What would have caused the Galatians to lose sight of these riches? Why do Christians today miss them?

From the Commentary

> To be "fallen from grace" does not mean to lose salvation.
> Rather, it means "fallen out of the sphere of God's grace."
> You cannot mix grace and law. If you decide to live in the
> sphere of law, then you cannot live in the sphere of grace.
> The believers in Galatia had been *bewitched* by the false
> teachers (Gal. 3:1) and thus were *disobeying* the truth.
> They had *removed* toward another gospel (1:6–9) and had
> *turned back* to the elementary things of the old religion
> (4:9).
>
> —*Be Free*, page 120

7. Circumcision was the most basic symbol of being Jewish rather than
Greek. Why might the Galatians have feared that God wouldn't be fully
happy with them unless they took on such practices? What did God want
from them instead (5:6), and why is that so much more important to Him?

From the Commentary

> Paul was fond of athletic illustrations and used them often
> in his letters. His readers were familiar with the Olympic
> Games as well as other Greek athletic contests that always
> included footraces. It is important to note that Paul never
> uses the image of the race to tell people how to be saved.
> He is always talking to Christians about how to live the
> Christian life. *A contestant in the Greek games had to be a*
> *citizen before he could compete.*
>
> —*Be Free*, page 121

8. How is running a race (5:7) a good metaphor to symbolize living the
Christian life? How is it possible to pursue our goal with an athlete's
discipline and yet with grace and faith?

From the Commentary

> Yeast is really a good illustration of sin: It is small, but
> if left alone it grows and permeates the whole. The false
> doctrine of the Judaizers was introduced to the Galatian

churches in a small way, but before long, the "yeast" grew and eventually took over.

—*Be Free*, page 122

9. What was the "yeast" that Paul was referring to in Galatians 5:9? What are some of the negative things in today's church that act as yeast? Why do you think Paul speaks such strong words to the "agitators" in Galatians 5:12? What sort of teachings common in today's church might prompt a similar passionate response?

From the Commentary

God's grace is sufficient for every demand of life. We are saved by grace (Eph. 2:8–10), and we serve by grace (1 Cor. 15:9–10). Grace enables us to endure suffering (2 Cor. 12:9). It is grace that strengthens us (2 Tim. 2:1) so that we can be victorious soldiers. Our God is the God of *all* grace (1 Peter 5:10). We can come to the throne of grace and find grace to help in every need (Heb. 4:16). As we read the Bible, which is "the word of his grace" (Acts 20:32), the Spirit of grace (Heb. 10:29) reveals to us how rich we are in Christ.

—*Be Free*, pages 123–24

10. What role does God's grace play in Paul's response to the Galatian Christians who were led astray? Where does Paul's confidence that the Galatians will "take no other view" come from?

Looking Inward

Take a moment to reflect on all that you've explored thus far in this study of Galatians 5:1–12. Review your notes and answers and think about how each of these things matters in your life today.

Tips for Small Groups: To get the most out of this section, form pairs or trios and have group members take turns answering these questions. Be honest and as open as you can in this discussion, but most of all, be encouraging and supportive of others. Be sensitive to those who are going through particularly difficult times and don't press people to speak if they're uncomfortable doing so.

11. In what ways do you feel "set free" by Christ? How have you lived out that freedom in the day-to-day? What are some of the things that threaten to keep you yoked to slavery? Why are you drawn to these things? What does the gospel of grace have to say about these things?

12. How have you been "running a good race" in your faith life? If you've been tripped up in the past, what caused that? What are some practical steps you can take to minimize the chances of being tripped up by these things again?

13. How can you focus on "faith expressing itself through love" (Gal. 5:6)? What are some practical things you can do? What do you need the Holy Spirit to do in you in order for this to permeate your way of life, and how can you cooperate with that process?

Going Forward

14. Think of one or two things that you have learned that you'd like to work on in the coming week. Remember that this is all about quality, not quantity. It's better to work on one specific area of life and do it well than to work on many and do poorly (or to be so overwhelmed that you simply don't try).

Do you let go of the things that keep you yoked to slavery? Do you better express your faith through love? Be specific. Go back through Galatians 5:1–12 and put a star next to the phrase or verse that is most encouraging to you. Consider memorizing this verse.

Real-Life Application Ideas: Take inventory of all the things you do to grow closer to Christ. This could be anything from regular prayer or Bible reading to leading worship in church services. What is your motivation for doing each of these things? How could any of these things become a yoke of slavery? What precautions do you need to take so you continue running the good race? Consider finding a mentor who can help you evaluate your motives for the things you do that are intended to grow your relationship with Christ.

Seeking Help

15. Write a prayer below (or simply pray one in silence), inviting God to work on your mind and heart in those areas you've previously noted. Be honest about your desires and fears.

Notes for Small Groups:

- *Look for ways to put into practice the things you wrote in the Going Forward section. Talk with other group members about your ideas and commit to being accountable to one another.*

- *During the coming week, ask the Holy Spirit to continue to reveal truth to you from what you've read and studied.*

- *Before you start the next lesson, read Galatians 5:13–26. For more in-depth lesson preparation, read chapter 10, "The Fifth Freedom," in* Be Free.

Free from Sin
(GALATIANS 5:13–26)

Before you begin …
- *Pray for the Holy Spirit to reveal truth and wisdom as you go through this lesson.*
- *Read Galatians 5:13–26. This lesson references chapter 10 in* Be Free. *It will be helpful for you to have your Bible and a copy of the commentary available as you work through this lesson.*

Getting Started

From the Commentary

Man needs to be free from himself and the tyranny of his sinful nature.

The legalists thought they had the answer to the problem in laws and threats, but Paul has explained that no amount of legislation can change man's basic sinful nature. It is not law on the *outside*, but love on the *inside* that makes the difference. We need another power within, and that power comes from the Holy Spirit of God.

—*Be Free,* page 127

1. Underline Paul's summary of the law (Gal. 5:14). Why do you think Paul chooses to underscore this truth in the context of his warning not to use freedom to indulge the sinful nature? How does the law fall short in preventing people from destroying each other (Gal. 5:15)?

More to Consider: Go through Galatians and circle any references Paul makes to the Holy Spirit. What does what you've circled tell you about the role of the Holy Spirit in the gospel of grace?

2. Choose one verse or phrase from Galatians 5:13–26 that stands out to you. This could be something you're intrigued by, something that makes you uncomfortable, something that puzzles you, something that resonates with you, or just something you want to examine further. Write that here.

Going Deeper

From the Commentary

> We are prone to go to extremes. One believer interprets
> *liberty* as *license* and thinks he can do whatever he wants to
> do. Another believer, seeing this error, goes to an opposite
> extreme and imposes law on everybody. Somewhere
> between *license* on the one hand and *legalism* on the other
> hand is true Christian liberty.
>
> —*Be Free*, page 128

3. How can Christians know if they're interpreting liberty as license? What
sorts of "checks and balances" need to be in place so believers don't swing
to either of the extremes (license or law)? What role does the Holy Spirit
play in this? Scripture? The church? Other believers?

From the Commentary

> Paul began by explaining *our calling:* We are called to
> liberty. The Christian is a free man. He is free from the
> *guilt* of sin because he has experienced God's forgiveness.

He is free from the *penalty* of sin because Christ died for him on the cross. And he is, through the Spirit, free from the *power* of sin in his daily life. He is also free from the *law* with its demands and threats. Christ bore the curse of the law and ended its tyranny once and for all.

—*Be Free*, page 128

4. What makes the prospect of freedom appealing to people today? What freedoms are people crying out for? How can freedom in Christ answer what lies at the core of those longings? To what extent do you think Christians today value freedom from sin's power, not just from sin's guilt and penalty? Why is that?

From the History Books

The countercultural movement in the 1960s was all about "freedom." Rebelling against the conservative culture of the time, the generation is marked by antiwar demonstrations, the rise of feminism, stretching the limits of the right to free speech, the popularization of the drug culture, and something that became known as "free love." During this turbulent period, tensions arose between those championing the causes of freedom and those intent on maintaining the status quo. This led to a number of violent skirmishes between the two groups, including the Kent State shootings in 1970.

5. What do you think sparked the "revolution" of the 1960s? What does that generation's understanding of freedom say about the people involved? How is the cry for freedom that echoed during that decade like or unlike the freedom offered through a relationship with Christ?

From the Commentary

> The amazing thing about love is that it takes the place of all the laws God ever gave. "Thou shalt love thy neighbor as thyself" solves every problem in human relations.
>
> —*Be Free*, page 129

6. What makes the message of Galatians 5:14 particularly important to the Galatian Christians in light of the confusion brought about by the false teachers? How does a "love your neighbor" philosophy mesh with Paul's strong words about those who are preaching falsely?

From the Commentary

> Just as Isaac and Ishmael were unable to get along, so the
> Spirit and the flesh (the old nature) are at war with each
> other. By "the flesh," of course, Paul did not mean "the
> body." The human body is not sinful; it is neutral. If the
> Holy Spirit controls the body, then we walk in the Spirit;
> but if the flesh controls the body, then we walk in the
> lusts (desires) of the flesh. The Spirit and the flesh have
> different appetites, and this is what creates the conflict.
>
> —*Be Free*, page 130

7. Go through Galatians 5:16–26 and circle all the things that the Spirit-
controlled life produces. Then underline Paul's list of sinful acts. How
might someone under the law respond to both of these lists? How would
they attempt to deal with the sins? Produce the fruit?

From the Commentary

> The solution is not to pit our will against the flesh, but
> to surrender our will to the Holy Spirit. This verse [5:18]

literally means "But if you are *willingly led* by the Spirit, then you are not under the law." The Holy Spirit writes God's law on our hearts (Heb. 10:14–17; see 2 Cor. 3) so that we *desire* to obey Him in love.

—*Be Free*, page 131

8. What does it look like to surrender our will to the Holy Spirit? (See Gal. 5:25.) How does the Holy Spirit Himself help make this possible? What are the greatest obstacles to this sort of surrender?

More to Consider: Galatians 5:19–21 describes three different categories of sin. What are these categories? Why do you think Paul makes special mention of these categories?

From the Commentary

It is one thing to overcome the flesh and *not do* evil things, but quite something else *to do* good things. The legalist might be able to boast that he is not guilty of adultery or murder (but see Matt. 5:21–32), but can anyone see the beautiful graces of the Spirit in his life? Negative goodness is not enough in a life; there must be positive qualities as well.

—Be Free, page 134

9. How does the Spirit enable believers to produce fruit? What does the term *fruit* imply that we might miss if Paul had said "works of the Spirit"? What are the personal and spiritual benefits of producing fruit instead of simply doing good works?

From the Commentary

It is possible for the old nature to *counterfeit* some of the fruit of the Spirit, but the flesh can never *produce* the fruit of the Spirit. One difference is this: When the Spirit produces fruit, God gets the glory and the Christian is not conscious of his spirituality; but when the flesh is at work, the person is inwardly proud of himself and is pleased when others compliment him. The work of the Spirit is to make us more like Christ for His glory, not for the praise of men.

Fruit grows in a climate blessed with an abundance of the Spirit and the Word.

—*Be Free*, page 136

10. How does God get the glory when people produce the fruit of the Spirit? Is it possible for those who are producing fruit to experience pride in that? If so, how does this happen? How can Christians avoid the sin of pride?

Looking Inward

Take a moment to reflect on all that you've explored thus far in this study of Galatians 5:13–26. Review your notes and answers and think about how each of these things matters in your life today.

Tips for Small Groups: To get the most out of this section, form pairs or trios and have group members take turns answering these questions. Be honest and as open as you can in this discussion, but most of all, be encouraging and supportive of others. Be sensitive to those who are going through particularly difficult times and don't press people to speak if they're uncomfortable doing so.

11. What specific challenges have you faced as you've attempted to live in freedom by the Holy Spirit, rather than by law? Do you still face those challenges today? How do you deal with them?

12. What are some ways you've used your freedom to indulge in sinful things? Why is it so easy to follow the sinful paths? How does the leading of the Spirit help keep you from choosing the sinful paths? What does it mean to you to surrender your will to the Spirit? How does that affect the decisions you make?

13. What are some of the ways you've struggled with pride? How can you tell when you're performing works driven by pride or fear instead of bearing fruit?

Going Forward

14. Think of one or two things that you have learned that you'd like to work on in the coming week. Remember that this is all about quality, not quantity. It's better to work on one specific area of life and do it well than to work on many and do poorly (or to be so overwhelmed that you simply don't try).

Do you need to work on being led by the Spirit instead of the flesh? Do you need to work on pride issues? Be specific. Go back through Galatians 5:13–26 and put a star next to the phrase or verse that is most encouraging to you. Consider memorizing this verse.

Real-Life Application Ideas: Take a look at Paul's "fruit of the Spirit" list and spend time in prayer asking God to help you follow Jesus' command to "Love your neighbor as yourself." Then take an inventory of your current relationships, examining the fruit that is in evidence in each of those relationships. If you discover you're bearing much fruit, be thankful! If you find areas where you are not bearing fruit, ask God to redirect you as necessary so you can begin doing so.

Seeking Help

15. Write a prayer below (or simply pray one in silence), inviting God to work on your mind and heart in those areas you've previously noted. Be honest about your desires and fears.

Notes for Small Groups:

- *Look for ways to put into practice the things you wrote in the Going Forward section. Talk with other group members about your ideas and commit to being accountable to one another.*

- *During the coming week, ask the Holy Spirit to continue to reveal truth to you from what you've read and studied.*

- *Before you start the next lesson, read Galatians 6. For more in-depth lesson preparation, read chapters 11 and 12, "The Liberty of Love" and "The Marks of Freedom," in* Be Free.

Love One Another
(GALATIANS 6)

Before you begin …
- *Pray for the Holy Spirit to reveal truth and wisdom as you go through this lesson.*
- *Read Galatians 6. This lesson references chapters 11 and 12 in* Be Free. *It will be helpful for you to have your Bible and a copy of the commentary available as you work through this lesson.*

Getting Started

From the Commentary

"One another" is one of the key phrases in the Christian's vocabulary. "Love one another" is found at least a dozen times in the New Testament, along with "pray one for another" (James 5:16), "edify one another" (1 Thess. 5:11), prefer one another (Rom. 12:10), "use hospitality one to another" (1 Peter 4:9), and many other like admonitions.

In the section before us, Paul adds another phrase: "Bear ye one another's burdens" (Gal. 6:2). The Spirit-led Christian thinks of others and how he can minister to them.

—*Be Free,* page 141

1. What does it mean to carry each other's burdens (Gal 6:2)? How does this fulfill the law of Christ?

More to Consider: Read Matthew 18:15–35. How does this mirror what Paul wrote in Galatians 6:1?

2. Choose one verse or phrase from Galatians 6 that stands out to you. This could be something you're intrigued by, something that makes you uncomfortable, something that puzzles you, something that resonates with you, or just something you want to examine further. Write that here.

Going Deeper

From the Commentary

> There is no contradiction between Galatians 6:2 and 5, because two different Greek words for *burden* are used. In Galatians 6:2 it is a word meaning "a heavy burden," while in Galatians 6:5 it describes "a soldier's pack." We should help one another bear the heavy burdens of life, but there are personal responsibilities that each man must bear for himself. "Each soldier must bear his own pack." If my car breaks down, my neighbor can help drive my children to school, but he cannot assume the responsibilities that only belong to me as their father.
>
> —*Be Free*, page 145

3. How do you know when a burden is something that needs to be shared and when it's simply a part of everyday life (the "soldier's pack")? What sorts of problems in the church would have prompted Paul to include mentions of both sorts of burdens in this letter to the Galatians? What are the dangers of trying to carry your heavy burdens alone? What happens to those who don't take responsibility for their lighter, everyday burdens?

From the Commentary

> God does not command believers to give simply that
> pastors and teachers (and missionaries, Phil. 4:10–19)
> might have their material needs met, *but that the givers*
> *might get a greater blessing* (Gal. 6:7–8). The basic principle
> of sowing and reaping is found throughout the entire
> Bible. God has ordained that we *reap what we sow*. Were
> it not for this law, the whole principle of cause and effect
> would fail. The farmer who sows wheat can expect to reap
> wheat. If it were otherwise, there would be chaos in our
> world.
>
> But God has also told us to be careful *where we sow,* and it
> is this principle that Paul dealt with [in Galatians 6:6–10].
>
> —*Be Free*, page 146

4. How does the principle of cause and effect play out in the circumstances
experienced by the Galatian Christians (some of whom were following false
teaching)? How do you see this (in both good and bad ways) in today's
church?

From Today's World

With the ready access to news provided by both television and the Internet, stories about a celebrity or other public figure's misfortunes are known literally within minutes of the event. There is little room for anyone in the public eye to make an error, lest they get caught on tape and suddenly find their indiscretion viewed by millions around the globe. In some ways, this forces people who are trying to make a good impression to step carefully. But for some, the added publicity does little to dissuade them from repeating the actions that brought unwarranted attention.

5. In what ways does popular culture today uphold the "sowing and reaping" principle outlined in Galatians? In what ways does it challenge that principle? What happens when people are not held responsible for what they sow? How is this different in secular culture than in the economy of God?

From the Commentary

> Sharing blessings involves much more than teaching the Word and giving of our material substance. It also involves doing good "unto all men" (Gal. 6:10).
>
> —*Be Free*, page 148

6. Read Luke 6:32–35. How does this passage support Paul's message in Galatians 6:9–10? What does Hebrews 13:16 tell us about a Christian's good works? How are these "good works" different than the works Paul speaks against elsewhere in Galatians? What is the motivation for doing good "unto all men"?

From the Commentary

> It was Paul's custom, after dictating a letter, to take the pen and write his own farewell. His standard signature was "The grace of our Lord Jesus Christ be with you" (1 Thess. 5:28; see 2 Thess. 3:17–18). But so concerned was Paul that the Galatians get the message of this letter that he took the pen and wrote *an entire concluding paragraph* with his own hand. "Look at the large letters I write with my own hand!"
>
> —*Be Free*, page 153

7. How is it significant that Paul wrote an entire paragraph in his own hand in big letters? What do you notice about the paragraph he chose to convey this way?

From the Commentary

Paul did not have anything good to say about the legalist. He described him and his kind in four ways.

(1) They are braggarts (6:12a, 13b).

(2) They are compromisers (6:12b).

(3) They are persuaders (6:12a).

(4) They are hypocrites (6:13).

—*Be Free*, pages 154–56

8. Why did Paul choose to close his letter with repeated strong words against the legalists? How does his disparaging depiction of them in 6:12–13 work in concert with his earlier exhortation to "do good to all people, especially to those who belong to the family of believers" (6:10)?

More to Consider: Paul keeps coming back to the cross in Galatians. (See 2:20–21; 3:13; 4:5; 5:11, 24; 6:12.) Why did Paul spend so much time focused on the cross, glorying in our redemption through Christ in light of the challenges the Galatian church was facing?

From the Commentary

For Paul, the cross meant *liberty*: from self (Gal 2:20), the flesh (5:24), and the world (6:14). In the death and resurrection of Christ the power of God is released to give believers deliverance and victory. It is no longer *we* who live; it is Christ who lives in us and through us. As we yield to Him, we have victory over the world and the flesh. There is certainly no power in the law to give a man victory over self, the flesh, and the world. Quite the contrary, the law *appeals* to the human ego ("I can do something to please God") and encourages the flesh to work.

—*Be Free*, page 157

9. In what ways has Paul been true to his desire to boast only "in the cross of our Lord Jesus Christ" (Gal. 6:14)? What is the difference between boasting in selfish things and boasting in the cross of Christ?

From the Commentary

There was a time when Paul was proud of his mark of circumcision (Phil. 3:4–6), but after he became a believer, he became a "marked man" in a different way. He now gloried in the scars he had received and in the suffering he had endured in the service of Jesus Christ.

The contrast with the legalists is plain to see: "The Judaizers want to mark your flesh and brag about you, but I bear in my body the brands of the Lord Jesus Christ—for His glory." What a rebuke! "If your religious celebrities have any scars to show for the glory of Christ, then let them be shown. Otherwise—stop bothering me!"

—*Be Free*, page 159

10. What are the "brands" that Christians sometimes wear today (apart from the mark of Christ)? Why did Paul write, "Let no one cause me trouble, for I bear on my body the marks of Jesus" (Gal. 6:17)? How are Christians today marked by Christ? What do those scars look like?

Looking Inward

Take a moment to reflect on all that you've explored thus far in this study of Galatians 6. Review your notes and answers and think about how each of these things matters in your life today.

Tips for Small Groups: To get the most out of this section, form pairs or trios and have group members take turns answering these questions. Be honest and as open as you can in this discussion, but most of all, be encouraging and supportive of others. Be sensitive to those who are going through particularly difficult times and don't press people to speak if they're uncomfortable doing so.

11. In what ways have you helped to carry others' heavy burdens? When have others helped you with your burdens? Have there been times when you didn't even want to carry your "soldier's pack" (your responsibilities)? What prompted that? How did you overcome that season?

12. What are some ways you're doing good "unto all men"? What is your motivation for doing these things? If your motivations are selfish, how can you refocus them so they're Christ-honoring?

13. What does the cross mean to you? How does Christ's sacrifice brand you? What scars do you bear because of your relationship with Jesus?

Going Forward

14. Think of one or two things that you have learned that you'd like to work on in the coming week. Remember that this is all about quality, not quantity. It's better to work on one specific area of life and do it well than to work on many and do poorly (or to be so overwhelmed that you simply don't try).

Do you need to reach out more to help others with their burdens? Do you need to learn how to better sow from the Spirit instead of selfishly? Be specific. Go back through Galatians 6 and put a star next to the phrase or verse that is most encouraging to you. Consider memorizing this verse.

Real-Life Application Ideas: Make this coming week a "carrying burdens" week. Ask family, friends, and others how you can help them with the challenges they're facing. These could be physical challenges, spiritual challenges, or even emotional challenges. Offer a helping hand or a listening ear and spend time with those in need. Do all of these things for the glory of God and not for any selfish gain.

Seeking Help

15. Write a prayer below (or simply pray one in silence), inviting God to work on your mind and heart in those areas you've previously noted. Be honest about your desires and fears.

Notes for Small Groups:
- *Look for ways to put into practice the things you wrote in the Going Forward section. Talk with other group members about your ideas and commit to being accountable to one another.*
- *During the coming week, ask the Holy Spirit to continue to reveal truth to you from what you've read and studied.*

Summary and Review

Notes for Small Groups: This session is a summary and review of this book. Because of that, it is shorter than the previous lessons. If you are using this in a small-group setting, consider combining this lesson with a time of fellowship or a shared meal.

Before you begin ...
- *Pray for the Holy Spirit to reveal truth and wisdom as you go through this lesson.*
- *Briefly review the notes you made in the previous sessions. You will refer back to previous sections throughout this bonus lesson.*

Looking Back

1. Over the past eight lessons, you've examined Paul's letter to the Galatians. What expectations did you bring to this study? In what ways were those expectations met?

2. What is the most significant personal discovery you've made from this study?

3. What surprised you most about Paul's comparison of "law" and "grace"? About Paul's obvious passion to respond to the false teachers?

Progress Report

4. Take a few moments to review the Going Forward sections of the previous lessons. How would you rate your progress for each of the things you chose to work on? What adjustments, if any, do you need to make to continue on the path toward spiritual maturity?

5. In what ways have you grown closer to Christ during this study? Take a moment to celebrate those things. Then think of areas where you feel you still need to grow and note those here. Make plans to revisit this study in a few weeks to review your growing faith.

Things to Pray About

6. Galatians is a deeply theological book, but it also includes plenty of practical application for growing or struggling Christians. As you reflect on the words Paul has written, ask God to reveal to you those truths that you most need to hear. Revisit the book often and seek the Holy Spirit's guidance to gain a better understanding of what it means to be righteous before God.

7. The messages in Galatians include law vs. grace, liberty vs. license, and learning to bear fruit in the Spirit. Spend time praying for each of these topics.

8. Whether you've been studying this in a small group or on your own, there are many other Christians working through the very same issues you discovered when examining Paul's letter to the Galatians. Take time to pray for each of them, that God would reveal truth, that the Holy Spirit would guide you, and that each person might grow in spiritual maturity according to God's will.

A Blessing of Encouragement

Studying the Bible is one of the best ways to learn how to be more like Christ. Thanks for taking this step. In closing, let this blessing precede you and follow you into the next week while you continue to marinate in God's Word:

May God light your path to greater understanding as you review the truths found in the book of Galatians and consider how they can help you grow closer to Christ.